For Kate
a love story in four parts

poems by
Rachael Ikins

For Kate: A Love Story in Four Parts

Clare Songbirds Publishing House Chapbook Series
ISBN 978-1-947653-11-5
Clare Songbirds Publishing House
For Kate © 2017 Rachael Ikins
All Rights Reserved. Clare Songbirds Publishing House retains right to reprint.
Permission to reprint individual poems must be obtained from the author who owns the copyright.

Printed in the United States of America
FIRST EDITION

Clare Songbirds Publishing House Mission Statement:
Clare Songbirds Publishing House was established to provide a print forum for the creation of limited edition, fine art from poets and writers, both established and emerging. We strive to reignite and continue a tradition of quality, accessible literary arts to the national and international community of writers, and readers. Chapbook manuscripts and art quality poetry broadsides are carefully chosen for their ability to propel the expansion of art and ideas in literary form. We provide an accessible way to promote the art of words in order to resonate with, and impact, readers not yet familiar with the siren song of poets and writers. Clare Songbirds Publishing House espouses a singular cultural development where poetry creates community and becomes commonplace in public places.

Clare Songbirds Publishing House
140 Cottage Street
Auburn, New York 13021
www.ClareSongbirdspub.com

Contents

Cats Only: Reminiscence with Nestle	9
David's Cats	10
Cat	11
Girlie	13
For Kate	16
Dawn Journeys	17
Perfection	19
Fear of Flying: Recue	22
Kitten	23
A Naughty Tale of Love in the Forest	24
Letter to My Birth Mom	27
Of Dragons and Other Mystical Guardians: a cat's night diary	28
A Possible Infidelity	29
Out of Orbit	32
What Can I Do	33
After Midnight	34
The Hardware Store Cat	37
Darkness	38

Acknowledgements

"David's Cats," "Kitten," "Hardware Store Cat" first appeared in *The Devon Rex Newsletter*, 1993

"Girlie" received Honorable Mention, CNY Chapter NLAPW Poetry Contest 2004, also on www.kjlyons.com 2004 and in *Slideshow in the Woods*, Foothills Publishing, 2008.

"For Kate" Poem of the Week, 2014 NLAPW.org and *Lost Horizon Cats Anthology,* 2014

"Dawn Journeys" and "Fear of Flying," first published in *Lost Horizon Cats Anthology,* 2014

"Fear of Flying," *Breath and Shadow*, 2015

"Of Dragons and Other Mystical Guardians," *Dragon Poet Review*, University of OK, 2016

All photos contained in this book are by Rachael Ikins © 2017

For Dr. Bob Upholt
who was there when Nestle left,
who gave Katie & me 2 extra years

and for Laura Wolfe
for bringing Leonard and Cato
to pick up the thread

"More than diamonds, more than gold-
--I ain't got much but I got you, baby"
Cheap Thrills, Sia

Part 1
Prelude

I was lucky enough to be born into a family of 3 cats. There were 2 humans too, but my earliest tactile memory is of a cat licking my hand in bed. At age 8, 3rd grade I was allowed to have my own kitten, chosen by me, and she was permitted to raise one litter of kittens before we spayed her. She died when I was away at college, both of us 18 years old, Spring in my mom's flower bed. Not a bad place to pass.

It wasn't until my early 40s that a cat came into my life who probably saved me. To this day I believe she was an angel and was sent in the only form I would respond to. I was very ill, lost to medications, side effects and adverse reactions. Nestle almost died 3 times and when after each recovery she beat odds, she amazed everyone. Though she was only 7 years old when she actually crossed the rainbow bridge, I'd understood that we were soulmates long before.

I had never experienced such a loss- and I had lost human family members- as when Nestle died. In some fundamental and profound new way I understood grief and that when a heart breaks, there is no glue.

I became a cat rescue person. My husband and I adopted over 19 cats and kittens during the course of our marriage. A kitten indirectly was the thing that brought us together in the first place. He telephoned me to tell that one of his elderly cats was gone. A couple in my apartment complex had a mother cat with a new litter. I chose a kitten for him.
I spent time after Nestle's death, sitting in the SPCA in the cat play room, petting homeless cats, tears rolling down my face. I've never forgotten a huge, 9 year old male tabby named "Tank" who had lost his human and home. We shared our grief, and I gave him what love I could relieved to have a place to go with my pain. Not to be alone with it.

After searching the internet for cat lovers, breeders, shelters, anyone to share my loss with, I began corresponding with a woman who lived down south. When I looked at photos of her kittens on her website, my eyes welled up, for in the depths of my despair I felt that here must be one who could help heal my bottomless pain. The breeder and I became email pals and long story short, one of her females was expecting two days after Nestle's birthday. Impulsively I sent her a deposit as soon as they were born because she had said she had a long waiting list. Thus Katie, first called "Dawn" by the little boys whose house she and her litter mates shared flew into my life on July 3, 2002 just under the heat embargo, coming from Georgia to Syracuse, NY at 10:00 p.m.

When Katie was 3 years old, we lost our house, filed for bankruptcy; and my husband was dealing with cancer, heart disease and dementia. We found ourselves in a small drafty, flimsy country cottage. It was a dark time. One afternoon I emailed with my southern friend and asked her if she could send me Katie's lineage as far back as she could. Katie and Nestle were the Devon Rex breed, with curly hair and "ET" faces, 6- 7 lbs. full grown. Nestle was a chocolate smoke, gray tail, brown ears and face, Katie was seal point. She replied "Sure."
When it came into my inbox and I read down the generations of grandparents and greats, lo and behold Nestle's father was the multiple x removed great, great grandpa of both of Katie's parents. My head jerked up. I stared out into the woods.

I thought, "She has not left me. Nestle never left."

And while Katie was without question herself, our soul-deep bond grew beyond any love I have ever experienced for any other living soul. You can write me off as a crazy cat lady/poet, that is ok by me. My heart knows what it knows. Katie died at age 14 last year. This book is born of that loss and that love.

Cats Only: Reminiscence with Nestle

I sit in a room from the past.
Never thought I'd find myself here
again nor that I'd be welcomed.

He drones on about ear mites, wax
and cat allergies even as his big hands with
the familiar arthritic knuckles manipulate her small
body to investigate every fold & cranny.
Her pupils dilate, ears flatten.

I realize his face was the last you saw, his laughing
blue eyes, that slightly hooked nose. His voice, the last
you heard urging you to stay. You chose him

when it came your time to pass. Not me who loved
you with winged desperation, but this man. I remember
the threat of tears in his voice when he phoned to tell
me he had tried everything to save you. I remember.

So, I bring your great grand-daughter to offer to his hands.
Here, the last place you were alive.

He finishes his examination. Holds her neck in his hand

like a lily
or a chalice.

She stretches her paws, fans toes,
her pupils shrink. He cradles her like an infant.
Sometimes you get a second chance.

David's Cats

Big man.
Thatch of gray ponytail captured
by a bandanna, glasses, a bush of beard,

a guitar-strumming,
Viet Nam-damaged man.

Rescues cats.
What a sight, his house,
a newborn kitten finger-stroked,
eggshell between his callused palms.

He piles his Jeep with bags and cans of cat food.
Couple afternoons weekly he bumps over
the county dump's puddled road
for the cats nobody wants.
Sets humane traps sweetened with mackerel.
Sings Tom Petty to them on the drive to the vet's.
Ferals neutered, given vaccine's fighting chance

against rabies, feline AIDS, distemper.
A broken leg or abscess repaired.

He drives them back to the landfill, old bath towels
hooded over their crates. Leaves the gates unlatched, walks
away.
Jeep growls down the hill before they creep or explode out—
       Home.

They nest in tire wells and cardboard's sag.
David fills dented cake-pans,
       mounds of cat chow.

Everyone in these parts, neighbors to municipal government
respects
David's cats.

Cat

She is just a flower,
gladiolus, phaleonopsis, maybe
She is just a back-arching, tail-
waving cat.
A chest-low invitation.
She is just a want,
a welcome, spread petals
absorb afternoon sun-light.
Curling, curled inside-out
sun-glistening sticky
pistil ringed with stamens.

She is just a crying-out.
For the moth.
For the tongue.

I call to you with my throaty voice.

Girlie

I am just a pencil-stroke
of a cat, an abbreviation
sliding side-ways through
your barn door.
Hesitation marks on the snow,
is it suicide to go in?
I hear your voice
through the kitchen window.
I call to you
with my throaty voice.
I let you see me, but
I erase myself
when you come
too close.

Regard me upside down

Part 2
Loving

For Kate

Your hair smells like gin.
Crisp, of-the-forest, cold.
You spent a day hoarding
sunlight, posing on one
windowsill after another.
Washing yourself of winter.
You followed the light
east to west. By evening
you'd soaked so many
rays, you were gravid
with heat, gold, and
that juniper

scent. You hold my wrist
between your teeth, your
pupils, dark moons, your sky-
blue eyes. You do not break
skin. I push my face into
your flank. I cannot
resist you.

Dawn Journeys

You divide the drapes,
a comb, hanks of hair.
Slip without sound onto sill.

300 ways to welcome sun-
Bare your belly.
Spread your toes.
Reach your arms.

Regard me upside down,
twin blues blink.
You do not look away
when you descend,
pour onto my chest,
heated hot, smelling wild.

Dogs look away, wag, worry
about starting a fight.

You don't care what I want.
    (I want only you)
You transport me to your universe,
turquoise sky, midnight.

And hold me there.
You hold me as I fall into your eyes.
I do not even cry out when your claws
pierce my skin.

Perfection

After sun and full of joie de vivre
you clamber up my pillow stack.
Vibrating like an engine you lick
my chin raw purple if you can tease
me out of the pile. You unfold yourself
along my face.

You flop 6 pounds, tiptoed suede over my nose.
You purr, no color in your dark
new-moon eyes. You are so happy.
I have to laugh. I can't breathe with a nose
full of you. You fit exactly into
my elbow crook, my fingers
just long enough to tuck beneath
your paws.

washing yourself of winter

Part 3
A Memoir of Two Souls

Fear of Flying: Rescue

12 years ago almost-birthday.
Muggy July, heat embargo.
10 pm. My thighs stuck to vinyl.

Diesel fragrant air, tired tourists
rumpled in, jackets lumped on arms,
meandering toward Baggage Claim.

I watched them dwindle.
All my losses weighted my ribs,
my own stained satchel.

Corridors echoed,
hydraulic doors hissed at the night
like a frightened cat.
My thighs stuck to vinyl.

Does the airport stay open 24/7?

At "too late" p.m. a blue-suited man entered
a door from the tarmac.
He carried a white basket hung from one finger.
My thighs stung unstuck,

he smiled,
"Is this yours?"

I took your carrier, my heart, in my own two hands,
pressed my face, painful on metal to see.

Blue crocheted baby-blanket inside
two enormous ear-tips poking through.
This exact moment

I knew your wings;
that you had grabbed me
by my scruff,
would carry me high,
heal me of
my fear of flying
no matter how I squall.

Kitten

Tree-frog cat
perches on
my shoulder;

moon eyes,
radar cone ears.
Teeters three-legged
to pat at a night moth.
Her breath-held,
bow-hipped,
seven toed grip.
Or is she a gargoyle?

A Naughty Tale of Love in the Forest

There stands in the woods a House of Yellow Snow
where only the bravest adventurer dares go.
Exists in the realm ruled by Pussy-cat Queen.
Her name is "Po-Po" and she reigns supreme.
When her ire is irked there's much consternation,
her legendary temper said to cause conflagration.

Her principle foe is a feline named Cherie.
Acrobatic, gold eyes seven-toed feet pink berries.
Between the alphabet letters of "C" and of "E"
stalks another odd cat, corpulent's can be.
She is much wider than elastic, white Cherie,
and when asked how she likes her meals, she says
"often and very."

Charlotte's a lotta girl, a calico waddler.
hearing can-opener's song, she's no dawdler!
The Queen rules over all, both peasant and churl.
Piercing blue eyes and sleek Devon curls.
"They're all beneath me!" she growls from my chest,
Her favorite perch, tucked 'tween my breasts.

She washes my face with such rough tongue-lashing
by Dawn I've bruises like those from some bashing!
Monkey our sphynx, clueless, skeevy and bald,
his attitude studly, his reality un-balled.
Nothing he likes as much as a heater
or pad turned "High" on Erin's chest. Either!

The last day of his life the Queen did thus notice
he was ready for Heaven. She curled like a lotus
above and around him, sharing her heat
from the tips of his ears to her chocolate feet.

Lowrider the dachshund, our selective listener
"Bring that penis, silly dat-sun Mister!"
He checks his baggage often to make sure its still there
his anxiety frequent should he lose it somewhere.
Papi the rooster, likewise afflicted,
his pecking from Arturo

certainly no tickling.
He "batches" in the barn with his porcine brother,
Roosevelt pig and he both stigmatized as "other."

The hens and Bella and Vincent get laid
with alarming regularity—the piper is paid.
Maggie's our outdoor Princess of Whine,
an irritable, pugnacious, bossy girl-swine.
Roosevelt, the hen-pecked and Papi forsaken,
Cara our galloper and Annie's heart, taken.
Road-trips and deer poop all made her vomit
yet thirteen years later, let a deer poop? She's on it.
Willie's our shepherd a peke who herds cats,
let one escape and he pins it down flat.

Bella, the boxer, everyone's Old Mother
used to love to lave Monkey while under the covers.
But, she bade him "Adieu" in an unsentimental way,
now focuses her attention on Queen Po-Po's sway.

Washing that cutie from one end to the other:
Fickle is the world of the animal lover.

nose to tail with Sister

Letter to My Birth Mom

A Feline Perspective, Katie
Dear Mom,

I arrived safely in New York. Didn't like the cold dark ride in the cargo hold of the jet. The blanket Janet crocheted me helped. My human is a lot of work. She misses her old cat. She tries to hold her heart, not show me her sadness. She sleeps poorly. Difficult to curl up next to thrashing legs. You didn't tell me about that. I sit on her chest, wash her chin like you did to me when I was a kitten. I wash so hard, she's marked purple when she wakes up. Sometimes I bite. Hold a paw with claws. Purr her chin. She laughs. Calms her, like you showed me, who was boss when I was little. Six years now passed the way humans measure time. I like it when she pushes her lips back and forth across my belly's fur. I like her happy smell. She worships me and rightly so. She rides me on her shoulder. I'm her Goddess.

A Canine Perspective, Annie
Dear Mom,

When I first climbed in, I threw up in their car. In the city, I was afraid to go outside to pee so I used the cold air vent at the foot of the stairs. I grew up pretty large. My hair is thick and black. They left me outside in the back yard a lot as a guard. I was lonely. I was scared. I adore my girl. I know everything she thinks about. My tail wags when I read her thoughts. Her scent changes when her heart beats too fast. I bring her my dolly. I give her my belly to slow it. I keep an eye on her when we run the fields. No matter how fast or far I fly, I watch her. I'd lay my life down for her. In the road, the woods, no question or hesitation. I worship her. She is my Goddess.

Of Dragons and Other Mystical Guardians: a cat's night diary

When Mom settles the book
on her chest, I climb her collarbone.
It is night. Lamplight shines,
words she reads. One hand
strokes my spine, again and again.
I purr. I know she likes my purr so I purr
loud. Her fingers find their blind blunt
way along my ribs' paths,
my curled fur. I needle her neck-skin.
Not enough to bleed, she laughs," Ow!"
My dilated pupils erase eyes' blue, see midnight
monsters she cannot.

Page corner bent, place held, she slips her book
between pillows. Our bed is in an east corner,
this darkened room. Sister joins us. She gnaws
a rubber toy for 15 minutes. Her doggy relaxation.
Mom flips light switch. Moonlight flows
freed of boundary, window-half undraped.

I listen to Mom's heart bustle, a small strong mouse
that tunnels. Sometimes it pauses, nose, whiskers
tremble for threat. I prick her neck skin, one claw. Mouse-music
scampers on. I scent her dreams, her skin, slip off her chest,
back to back with her, nose to tail with Sister.
Mom curls, a sleep-wrought snail,
Sister and I, her shell.

She complains from night's deep dream when she wants
to leave the bed. A necessary acrobat, over and around us.
She does not know (wonderful human mother)
we are dragons sent by God
to protect her from the night.

A Possible Infidelity

I've seen your picture, lying across
your woman's poetry book, consider
yourself a god or at least a minor sun.
I backed up onto the computer screen so
my girl could no longer be tempted by you.

Yes, you are beautiful. I've known your kind.
My torn ear proves it. I loved a feline boy once.
named Irving. Curly hair, colored chocolate
and white. His ecstasy, I'd pin him down,
his throat-skin in my teeth. He smiled.
Winters, we hunkered on the register in the bathroom.
Furnace warmed our toes, our blood
rose. We sang praises, lust and hot planets.

You are not my lover. You are an alien
in my girl's lap-top.
I growl to ponder your golden eyes.

You cannot have her.
She belongs to me.
You cannot keep her.
Send her back to me, Puck.

No matter, when you meet,
you tolerate her touch, you notice
her fingers understand
the exact bones to scratch along your jaw,
behind ear's flare, transform a cat
into a rocket engine of desire.

I huddle in my window behind the drape,
hoarding sulky sun this Syracuse day.
I wonder if she slept, traveled moon's fullness
without me.
She'd better not
be sleeping with you.

you fit exactly

Part 4
Loss

Out of Orbit

A week since you died.
I take out the garbage,
wash laundry.
I buy food someone else
cooked and eat it.

Run the dishwasher,
shower.
I watch shows
read old books,
then crawl into our bed
each night wondering how
to curve my body so that
I don't disappear into the crater
left behind your passing.

All I want to do is sleep.
I can't sleep. You visit me at odd
times; I see you rounding the doorway
to my study, hear you digging in the plants.
The first Friday, one-week anniversary night,
both dogs in plain sight, felt you jump on the pillow
behind my head
while I read.

My hands fluttered
birds of joy
for you.

Sun still blushes every morning's sky.
I show your picture, tell your stories, but
I am a moon with no planet.

Shocked out of orbit,
I spin through firefly-lit darkness
amazed, stunned I cannot
find you.

What Can I do

The months walk away,
carry you on their shoulders.
Soon it will be a year since
the last blink of your blue eyes,
since I called to you "babygirl?"

He has found his way here,
blush where you were sable,
his eyes, lavender lights.
His name sounds like yours. Cato.
I can call out "Kate" again,
my heart comforted by saying it-
Kate, Kate, Cate. He is not you.

He was abandoned.
We share trust issues.
Where you
stapled yourself to my breastbone
guarding my heart,

he slams himself against my back
rearranging his body between my shoulder blades
pinching my skin in his teeth and clawed paws.
Overwhelmed with joy,
this closeness.
Both of us
needful.

After Midnight

You were not a carry-cat, nor a lapper.
You stood on my shoulders, you liked
a loose hand to steady your feet.
You loved my bath, an island survivor on my skin,
your tail in the water trailing, a mermaid's or a seaweed.
You always ended our day on my chest, until you crawled
beneath the covers, washed, to sleep against my hip.

How many nights I woke and reached for you?

I push my face into your blanket.
I look at photos and drawings of you.
It is only 10 am.

We traveled together, lived in seven cities.
Stayed with friends, strangers and my mother.
You were with me when she died.
When my husband died.
Through a second marriage and divorce,
in poverty and plenty, and
all the evenings I typed poetry
on my laptop
one-handed
because my other arm held
you
where you purred
under my chin.

Epilogue

Every year hundreds of thousands of unwanted cats are killed in shelters throughout the United States. Cats are tossed out of car windows into wooded areas or fields near farms as if the person doing it believes, if they even think about it, that a cat that has lived its entire life inside a human home, fed from cans and boxes of chow, perhaps even declawed (which is the barbaric removal of the first knuckle of the digit) will instantly know how to survive in the wild. Most die of starvation, dehydration or predation.

Too many cats are not spayed or neutered and one intact pair can multiply to 300 kittens within a few generations. There is no reason not to have this simple procedure done. There are organizations like Spay and Neuter Syracuse in Syracuse, NY which can help with the funds. For a while Katie and I lived in a small town in upstate New York. I was so amazed at the number of local businesses where a homeless cat or dog had found forever space to live. From the local library, a restaurant, to the hardware, the greenhouse/florist business on the corner to the antique shop, there was always a rescue cat ruling supreme. With human company all day, and safe inside and warm at night.

So, I end my tribute to Kate and many other four-footed family members who have walked these pages with you with a tribute to one of those businesses. Please, if you can, adopt don't shop. If you do choose a breeder, do your homework and pick someone who loves cats and treats them well, and gives them adequate hygiene, nutrition, health care and love. Make provisions in your will or health care proxy so that if you become ill or die suddenly, your pets have guardians in place. If you are allergic to cats but still love them, drop a couple of cans of cat food in the donations barrels a lot of pet stores have, or drop food or clean old towels and blankets at your local shelter instead of tossing them in the trash. If you live in Central New York, donate to the CNY Cat Coalition. Doesn't have to be a lot, but it can help save a life.

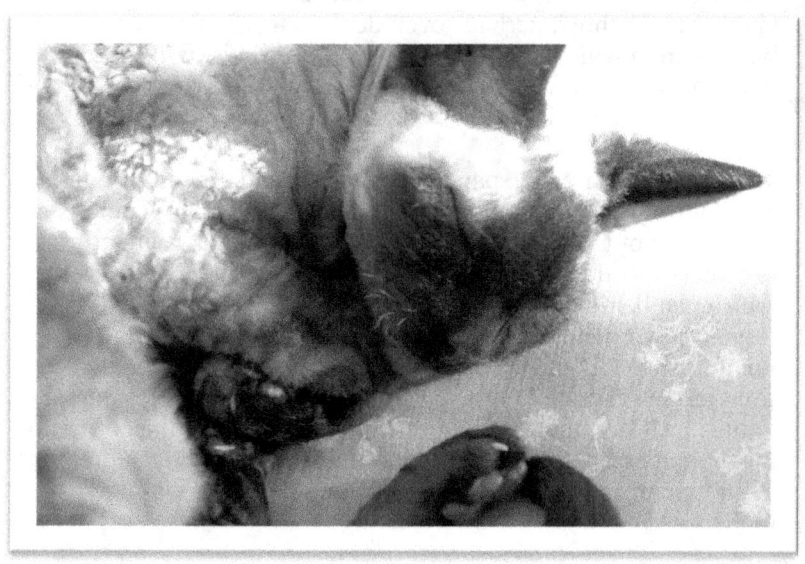

I cannot resist you

The Hardware Store Cat

He lives in the small
neighborhood hardware,
a Halloween orange tabby,
a mutt hound for company.
Rescues.

They guard the shop
from their pillow beds
through night's dreams,
neon cast shadows stripe
their bodies after humans leave.

Saturdays when I run down to pick
up caulk or paint, he sniffs my jeans' cuffs.
I stand still for him.
His mouth gapes, pupils flood his green
eyes dark—
tales my cats tell him
through my clothing.
Stories I know nothing about,
of that I am sure.

In the dry goods department,
a pile of new black Levis
sprinkled with yellow hairs
betrays his secret nap place.

He rolls his tabby
bulk on the counter
beneath the photograph
in memory of the previous beloved
hardware feline.
Next to the cash register,
he knocks pen cup and receipt stack
to the floor while I pay for my handful of bolts.
His upside down squint dares me. His paws reach.
Claws' promise. I say, "Good bye, Buddy."
Know not to touch
the hardware store cat.

Post Script

Darkness

Loafed in mulch beneath
the deck, an orange cat;
above his head, table,
two chairs, pumpkins, gourds and
glowing string lights. He stares,
just a jump away.
This place looks like "home."
Then he bundles
his bones into the woods.

Her favorite perch

Rachael Ikins is a 2016 & 2017 Pushcart, 2013 CNY Book Award nominee, and an award winning poet & artist. Her artwork has appeared in exhibits in Syracuse, Hamilton, and Albany, NY, as well as at the NYS Fair. Her writing has been published in journals around the world. She has been a featured poet/artist at Caffe Leana, Tyler Gallery, aaduna, and Palace Poetry. Rachael founded and moderated Monday Night Poetry at Sushi Blues and other regional poetry events. She has published six chapbooks, a full length eBook poetry collection, and a novel. The novel, Totems, is her first illustrated book. Rachael is a member of NLAPW. She belongs to Associated Artists of CNY and other guilds. She lives on Star Lake in Foxfire with her dogs, cats, and salt water fish tank filled with creatures that glow in the dark, many plants, books, and her garden.

The audiobook of *For Kate* will soon be available at
https://www.claresongbirdspub.com/shop/poetry/audiobooks/

www.ingramcontent.com/pod-product-compliance
Lightning Source LLC
Chambersburg PA
CBHW062040120526
44592CB00035B/1802